FINDING YOUR GRACE PLACE

RYAN REGER

For free updates to this book and for information related to
Finding Your Grace Place please go to
http://findingyourgraceplace.com/updates-info/

This book is dedicated to my amazing wife and best friend, Melane.

Melane, you have always encouraged me and supported me in my pursuit of my grace place and for that I am so grateful.

Table of Contents

Introduction

I believe that deep down inside every one of us there is a desire to take the talents and abilities we each have been blessed with to fulfill God's call on our life. For someone that doesn't know the Lord, they may not realize those talents are from Him, but they still have the desire to be all they can be as the US Army commercial said.

I submit to you that one cannot be truly happy if they are not doing what they were created to do. Dan Miller tells the story in his book *48 Days to the Work you Love* (A book I highly recommend you read) about an attorney who was never happy practicing law. In fact, he went through a period of sickness for 6 months that was triggered completely by stress. He wrote to Dan saying "I feel destined to do something great, but have no idea why or what. I work only for the money." (Miller 77)

Dan points to Ecclesiastes 5:10 which says:

> *"He who loves money will not be satisfied with money, nor he who loves abundance with its gain. This too is vanity (emptiness)."*

(All Scripture references in this book are from the Amplified version unless noted otherwise)

I can't say it any better so I'll quote Dan again - "Money is never enough compensation for investing our time and energy. There must be a sense of meaning, purpose, and accomplishment. Anything that does not blend our values, dreams, and passions will cause us on some level to choke. A life well lived must go beyond just making a paycheck – even if it's a very large one." (Miller 78)

Since about my teenage years the overarching prayer for my life has been that I would fulfill every purpose and plan God has for me. I want to be about His business as Jesus said in Luke 2:49:

"Did you not see and know that it is necessary [as a duty] for Me to be in My Father's house and [occupied] about My Father's business?"

When I get to Heaven I want to hear Him say "Well done thou good and faithful servant."

Who is this book for?

It's for the person that desperately wants to play the part God intended for them to play.

Or maybe you're the person that knows there is more for you in life, but aren't sure how to get there. Either way, hopefully by the end of this book you'll know that you are so loved by God and that He has an amazing plan for you and that you can walk out His plan for your life.

I don't care if you're 9 or 99, you can move in the direction of His calling for you.

You can do it.

You must do it.

There is a world out there that is desperate for the talent you have.

Let's do this.

Chapter 1

Jesus Loves You

Do you know what the most important thing is to God?

People.

You.

I know you have heard before that God loves you. If you grew up in church like I did, it's a statement that is hammered into you in Sunday School. It's an absolutely wonderful message, but it's just words until it becomes personal to you.

One of the best songs ever written in my opinion is "Jesus Loves Me". It's one you probably learned very early on in your life, but when is the last time you sang it?

Here are the words:

> *Jesus loves me this I know*
> *For the Bible tells me so*
> *Little ones to Him belong*
> *They are weak, but He is strong*
> *Yes, Jesus loves me*
> *Yes, Jesus loves me*
> *Yes, Jesus loves me*
> *The Bible tells me so*

I know this might seem silly, but I encourage you to sing it right now. If you're reading this in public just sing under your breath unless you want to get some funny looks.

Let the words wash over you. Think about what Jesus did for you at the cross as you sing it.

No matter where you are in your life right now.

No matter what you have done.

Jesus loves you so much!!

His love for you is so great, so inexhaustible.

Paul says in Romans 8:38,39:

> *"For I am convinced [and continue to be convinced—beyond any doubt] that neither death, nor life, nor angels, nor principalities, nor things present and threatening, nor things to come, nor powers, nor height, nor depth, nor any other created thing, will be able to separate us from the [unlimited] love of God, which is in Christ Jesus our Lord."*

Are you convinced of God's love for you?

You can be.

The key to becoming convinced of His love is to meditate on scriptures that talk about His love for you.

I'm sure you know John 3:16:

> *"For God so [greatly] loved and dearly prized the world, that He[even] gave His [One and] [a]only begotten Son, so that whoever believes and trusts in Him [as Savior] shall not perish, but have eternal life."*

Would you give your child for the sake of someone else?

I bet not. Most people wouldn't.

Yet God loves us so very much He sent His one and only Son, Jesus, to die for us so that we could have eternal life with Him. This isn't something we earn. It's a free gift.

Before we go any further, let me ask you – Have you received the free gift of Jesus Christ? Are you certain that if you died today you would go to Heaven?

You can be certain. Your eternity is not something to be left to chance.

If you would like to receive Jesus as your Savior then please pray this prayer with me:

> *Jesus, thank you for loving me and dying on the cross for me. I believe that your blood washes me clean of every sin – past, present, and future. I believe that you rose from the dead and that you are alive today. I receive you as my Lord and Savior. Because of your finished work on the cross, I am now a beloved child of God and Heaven is my home. Thank you for filling my heart with your peace and joy and giving me eternal life. Amen*

If you prayed that prayer, would you please do one more thing and send me an email at ryan@findingyourgraceplace.com?

You may be wondering why I'm talking about God's love for you in a book about fulfilling your call. The answer is that God's love is the foundation.

When you know the love God has for you, you can conquer any challenge life throws at you.

Look at the story of Jesus when he went to the Jordan River to be baptized. When the Holy Spirit descended like a dove what did the father say to Jesus?

> *"You are My beloved Son, in You I am well-pleased and delighted!"*

What happened to Jesus right after he was baptized?

Yes. He was led into the wilderness to be tempted by Satan.

And what did Satan preface every question with?

He asked "If you are the Son of God...."

I never saw this before until our pastor pointed this out, but do you see the words Satan left out of each of his questions?

"Beloved."

If you get this, this can make a HUGE difference in your life. Jesus was able to overcome every single one of Satan's attacks because He knew He was loved by His Father.

So what does knowing you're loved have to do with facing tough circumstances or fulfilling God's call on your life?

I'm so glad you asked.

When you know God loves you, you know He is for you. And when you know He is for you, you know there is no devil in hell that can stop you from fulfilling His call on your life and you walking in your grace place.

Romans 8:31,32 says:

> *"What then shall we say to [all] of this? If God is for us, who [can be] against us? [Who can be our foe if God is on our side]?*

Psalm 118:6 says:

> *"The Lord is on my side; I will not fear. What can man do to me?"*

I also love Hebrews 13:5,6 which says:

> *"[God] Himself has said, I will not in any way fail you nor give you up nor leave you without support. [I will] not, [I will] not, [I will] not in any degree leave you helpless nor forsake nor let [you] down (relax My hold on you)! [Assuredly not!]. So we take comfort and are encouraged and confidently and boldly say, The Lord is my Helper; I will not be seized with alarm [I will not fear or dread or be terrified]. What can man do to me?"*

Do you remember the story of David and Goliath? I bet even if you didn't grow up in Sunday School you know this story. It can be found in 1 Samuel 17.

What I bet you didn't know is that David's name in Hebrew means "Beloved."

David know he was loved by God, which gave Him the strength to defeat Goliath.

So to wrap up this chapter, let me say to you again – You are so dearly loved by our Heavenly Father.

There is nothing you have done or will ever do in your entire life that can stop Him from loving you.

Be conscious of His love for you. Make it a point to say "Jesus Loves Me."

Knowing He loves you will give you the power to overcome any obstacle you come across in your journey of finding and entering your grace place.

Chapter 2

What is a Grace Place?

So what is the title of this book all about?

To better answer that let's start with defining what grace is. It is a word you have probably heard many times, but do you know what it means?

Let's let Apostle Paul answer this from Romans 11:6 (NLT):

> *"And since it is through God's kindness, then it is not by their good works. For in that case, God's grace would not be what it really is — free and undeserved."*

And according to Webster's 1828 dictionary grace can be defined as − "Favor, good will, favorable influence of God, free unmerited love and favor of God."

So if we put these two together we get: The free and undeserved favor and love of God.

You don't deserve it and there's nothing you can do to earn it.

It's a free gift of God. It's simply our job to receive it.

The term "grace" is easy to understand in terms of our salvation.

Ephesians 2:8,9 (KJV) says:

> *"For by grace are ye saved through faith; and that not of yourselves: it is the gift of God: Not of works, lest any man should boast."*

Just as you were saved by the grace of God, that same grace can flow to every area of your life and in order to be effective for Him in those areas you desperately need His grace.

The way you receive it is simply the same way you did when you accepted Jesus as your Savior – you ask.

For me it's usually a prayer like "God, I can't do this on my own" or "I don't know what to do. Please Help."

Then what is a grace place?

Your grace place is the reason you were created, your calling. In Galatians 1:15 Paul describes being chosen from his mother's womb:

> "Who had chosen and set me apart [even] before I was born and had called me by His grace (His undeserved favor and blessing)"

It's by His grace because it's His ability within you that empowers you to fulfill it.

And your gifts, talents, and abilities point to your grace place and give you a clue as to what yours might be.

1 Peter 4:10 says:

> "Just as each one of you has received a special gift [a spiritual talent, an ability graciously given by God], employ it in serving one another as [is appropriate for] good stewards of God's multi-faceted grace [faithfully using the diverse, varied gifts and abilities granted to Christians by God's unmerited favor]."

Romans 12:6a says:

> "Having gifts (faculties, talents, qualities) that differ according to the grace given us, let us use them"

What are you really good at?

What comes natural to you?

Are there desires in your heart that have been there since you were young that you have yet to accomplish?

Let me give you an example from my own life – My wife and I have built a very successful business selling physical products online. Because of that success, I have had the privilege to teach others how to do the same thing through my books and courses.

Invariably, when someone meets me that has an interest in starting an online business they ask me questions. This is a topic I can spend hours talking about.

To me one of the greatest pleasures is helping others figure out how they can take their knowledge and skill set and turn it into a business.

I get excited for them and love to be able to help them see an opportunity they don't see for themselves. It energizes me to think through ideas with them and point them in the right direction.

What is it for you that energizes you?

What topic can you talk about for hours?

I know there are lots of great books and material out there about how to discover and fulfill God's purpose for your life. It's a desire most of us have – to find out why we're here on this Earth and to make the most of it and we'll dig deeper into how to find your grace place later, but I want to establish a foundation.

The main point I want to emphasize throughout this whole book is *to completely fulfill the calling God has for you you're going to have to completely rely on Him.*

I want to point you to Him and His grace. He is the one who gives you that special talent in the first place and anoints you to use it for Him.

Let's look at Romans 12:3. Paul says here:

"For by the grace (unmerited favor of God given to me) I warn everyone not to estimate and think of himself more highly than he ought."

In the King James version it reads "For I say, through the grace given unto me"

Why didn't Paul just say "I warn everyone"?

Why did he add in "For by the grace (unmerited favor of God given to me)" or in the King James version "through the grace given unto me"?

After meditating and praying over this scripture I believe the reason is Paul recognized that in order to do anything in his ministry he had to rely completely on the Lord.

If anyone could have relied on himself it would have been Paul. He was a smart guy.

In Philippians 3:5 he says:

"Circumcised when I was eight days old, of the race of Israel, of the tribe of Benjamin, a Hebrew [and the son] of Hebrews; as to the observance of the Law I was of [the party of] the Pharisees"

Although Paul was a Roman citizen, he was born of Hebrew stock and of the tribe of Benjamin. This meant as early as age six, Paul would have attended school in the synagogue where he would have been drilled in the scriptures and learned Hebrew.

"He was educated in Jerusalem and learned "at the feet" of his teacher (Acts 22:3), Rabbi Gamaliel who is believed to be one of the most brilliant of all teachers at that time. This could mean that Paul was a Rabbi which would explain why he was a member of the Pharisee's at one time"

(http://www.patheos.com/blogs/christiancrier/2014/08/14/who-was-the-apostle-paul/)

As he says himself in verse 4 of Philippians 3:

"Though for myself I have [at least grounds] to rely on the flesh. If any other man considers that he has or seems to have reason to rely on the flesh and his physical and outward advantages, I still have more!"

However back in verse 3 he says:

"For we [Christians] are the true circumcision, who worship God in spirit and by the Spirit of God and exult and glory and pride ourselves in Jesus Christ, and put no confidence or dependence [on what we are] in the flesh and on outward privileges and physical advantages and external appearances"

And in the next chapter he says in verse 13:

"I have strength for all things in Christ Who empowers me [I am ready for anything and equal to anything through Him Who infuses inner strength into me; I am self-sufficient in Christ's sufficiency]."

In 1 Corinthians 3:10 Paul says:

"According to the grace (the special endowment for my task) of God bestowed on me."

Grace produces the empowerment to do what you could not do on your own.

His grace working through you will produce the God kind of results.

Grace makes all the difference. Jesus makes all the difference.

If you're a confident person or very educated like the Apostle Paul, you might be tempted to think your own efforts will get you to your grace place. Or you might be on the other side of the fence and think you are not qualified to step into your grace place (I'll deal with you in the next chapter).

Both of those postures are focused on self-effort, which is the complete opposite of grace.

Remember, grace is the free and undeserved favor of God. You can't earn it. It's a free gift.

And in order to truly step into your grace place and have the God kind of results you have to rely on Him.

I love this section of Romans 12 in the Message Bible:

> "I'm speaking to you out of deep gratitude for all that God has given me, and especially as I have responsibilities in relation to you. Living then, as every one of you does, in pure grace, it's important that you not misinterpret yourselves as people who are bringing this goodness to God. No, God brings it all to you.
>
> The only accurate way to understand ourselves is by what God is and by what he does for us, not by what we are and what we do for him.
>
> In this way we are like the various parts of a human body.
>
> Each part gets its meaning from the body as a whole, not the other way around. The body we're talking about is Christ's body of chosen people. Each of us finds our meaning and function as a part of his body. But as a chopped-off finger or cut-off toe we wouldn't amount to much, would we? So since we find ourselves fashioned into all these excellently formed and marvelously functioning parts in Christ's body, let's just go ahead and be what we were made to be, without enviously or pridefully comparing ourselves with each other, or trying to be something we aren't."

The body of Christ, which is the church, needs you to step into your grace place.

The world needs you to step into your grace place.

As the scripture above says "let's go ahead and be what we were made to be."

My role is no less important than yours and your role is no less important than mine.

Let's completely rely on Him to step into our grace place.

Chapter 3

He has Qualified You

Many people think the attitude of "I'm not worthy" is being humble

If you're tempted to look at yourself and feel like there is no way God can use you or that you could ever step into your grace place let me challenge you in this chapter.

The truth is, alone you cannot. But you're not alone.

God Almighty, the Creator of the Universe is on your side (Romans 8:31).

Did you ever play sports? If so, do you remember the cheerleaders and the fans cheering for you?

Well, today I am your cheerleader and your coach.

You have too much to offer to sit on the sidelines. God has endowed you with unique talents and abilities the body of Christ and the world needs. I can't fill that role. You have to do it.

So think of this chapter as an injection of encouragement.

We started this book talking about God's love for you. His love for you is unshakeable. It's unconditional.

Unconditional means there is no sin you have committed to stop Him from loving you and there is no good thing you can do to earn it. It's there no matter what.

Romans 5:8 (NIV) says:

> *"But God demonstrates his own love for us in this: While we were still sinners, Christ died for us."*

To fully step into your grace place, your focus has to be on Him, on His love for you, on His grace.

Hebrews 12:2 says:

> *"Looking away from all that will distract to Jesus."*

Once you make a step toward your grace place, the devil will be there to tell you why you can't do it.

Some of the accusations may be:

You're not a perfect Christian.

You yelled at your wife yesterday.

You haven't read your Bible in a whole week.

You don't pray an hour a day like the other guy does.

You missed church two weeks in a row.

You lied on the application.

You had horrible thoughts toward that person.

Who are you to dream big? No one in your family has ever amounted to anything.

You have always been a failure.

And the lies will keep coming, but here is what I want you to do when those lies are being hurled at you – take the sword of the Spirit, which is the Word of God and speak it out loud.

The truth is:

You are qualified. Colossians 1:12 says:

> *"Who has qualified and made us fit"*

You are the righteousness of God in Christ. Romans 5:21 says:

"For our sake He made Christ [virtually] to be sin Who knew no sin, so that in and through Him we might become [endued with, viewed as being in, and examples of] the righteousness of God [what we ought to be, approved and acceptable and in right relationship with Him, by His goodness]."

You are completely forgiven. Psalm 103:12 says:

"As far as the east is from the west so far has He removed our transgressions from us."

Romans 8:1:

"There is therefore now no condemnation to them which are in Christ Jesus"

I could fill up a whole book with scriptures that speak of your forgiveness and your righteousness.

The point is, when the lies start coming latch on to those scriptures and fight back with your mouth.

If you can get a revelation of God's love for you and how completely forgiven and righteous you are because of Jesus then there's no stopping you.

So stop putting condemnation on yourself. God has forgiven you and removed all your sins as far as the east is from the west so forgive yourself, get back on your feet and move on.

You are a child of the Most High God and nothing you have done or ever will do can keep Him from loving you.

And furthermore, what you have done in the past does not disqualify you for stepping into your grace place. This is important. Let me say this again. There is nothing you have done in your past that can disqualify you from stepping into your grace place.

Romans 11:29 says:

"For God's gifts and His call are irrevocable. [He never withdraws them when once they are given, and He does not change His mind about those to whom He gives His grace or to whom He sends His call.]"

If you're still not convinced your past mistakes aren't stopping you from stepping into your grace place, let's look at the example of King David and just how awesome God's grace is.

David is well known for killing Goliath, but he made some huge mistakes or shall we say did some pretty awful things.

Let's look at 2 Samuel 11:1:

"In the spring, when kings go forth to battle, David sent Joab with his servants and all Israel, and they ravaged the Ammonites [country] and besieged Rabbah. But David remained in Jerusalem."

A whole sermon could be preached about that last sentence - "David remained in Jerusalem". He was where he wasn't supposed to be, which was out with his army. When you're somewhere you shouldn't be you're asking for trouble and that's exactly what David got.

Scripture continues to say:

"One evening David arose from his couch and was walking on the roof of the king's house, when from there he saw a woman bathing; and she was very lovely to behold.

David sent and inquired about the woman. One said, Is not this Bathsheba, the daughter of Eliam and the wife of Uriah the Hittite?

And David sent messengers and took her. And she came in to him, and he lay with her-for she was purified from her uncleanness. Then she returned to her house.

And the woman became pregnant and sent and told David, I am with child.

David sent to Joab, saying, Send me Uriah the Hittite. So Joab sent [him] Uriah.

When Uriah had come to him, David asked him how Joab was, how the people fared, and how the war progressed.

David said to Uriah, Go down to your house and wash your feet.

Uriah went out of the king's house, and there followed him a mess of food [a gift] from the king.

But Uriah slept at the door of the king's house with all the servants of his lord and did not go down to his house.

When they told David, Uriah did not go down to his house, David said to Uriah, Have you not come from a journey? Why did you not go down to your house?

Uriah said to David, The ark and Israel and Judah live in tents, and my lord Joab and the servants of my lord are camping in the open field. Shall I then go to my house to eat and drink and lie with my wife?

As you live and as my soul lives, I will not do this thing.

And David said to Uriah, Remain here today also, and tomorrow I will let you depart. So Uriah remained in Jerusalem that day and the next.

David invited him, and he ate with him and drank, so that he made him drunk; but that night he went out to lie on his bed with the servants of his lord and did not go down to his house.

In the morning David wrote a letter to Joab and sent it with Uriah.

And he wrote in the letter, Put Uriah in the front line of the heaviest fighting and withdraw from him, that he may be struck down and die.

So when Joab was besieging the city, he assigned Uriah opposite where he knew the enemy's most valiant men were.

And the men of the city came out and fought with Joab, and some of the servants of David fell. Uriah the Hittite died also."

You might have done some bad things in your life, but I bet you have never committed adultery with someone and then had their spouse killed. Don't get me wrong. Sin is sin. However we as humans tend to grade sins and in my grade book committing adultery with someone and having their spouse murdered is way worse than anything I have ever done.

The child that Bathsheba gave birth to died as God said it would, but did you know King Solomon was the son of Bathsheba?

Talk about some major restoration – the wisest, richest King that has ever lived was a son from an adulterous relationship that never should have happened.

What blows my mind even more is God chose for His son, Jesus, to be born in the line of Bathsheba!!!

Look at Matthew 1:6:

"Jesse the father of King David, King David the father of Solomon, whose mother had been the wife of Uriah."

Also, look at the previous verse "Salmon the father of Boaz, whose mother was Rahab."

Do you remember who Rahab was? She was the prostitute who was saved from death and destruction along with her family at Jericho because she hid the spies from Israel. (Joshua 2, 6)

So in the line of Jesus, we have a prostitute and an adulteress.

Isn't God's grace amazing?

I don't believe there are any insignificant details in the Bible. Look closely at verse 6 again. It says "whose mother had been the wife of Uriah." Why didn't God say "whose mother was Bathsheba"?

Why did he have to remind us that David did something very awful in having Uriah killed?

I believe it's to demonstrate how amazing his grace really is. It would have been easy for him to scrub the details of David's mistake under a rug, yet He chose Bathsheba's son to follow after David as king.

Even more, God decided He would have His son be born in this same line!

My friend, God can redeem any situation, any past mistake you have made.

Believe me when I tell you there is nothing you have done or ever will do to keep Him from loving you or that can disqualify you from stepping into your grace place.

Accept His love. Accept His forgiveness.

And step into your grace place.

Chapter 4

Jesus – Our Perfect Example

John 17:4 says:

> *"I have glorified You down here on the earth by completing the work that You gave Me to do."*

This is my life verse.

I love how the Message Translation words it:

> *"I glorified you on earth by completing down to the last detail what you assigned me to do."*

"The last detail." This is the prayer for my life, but I know there is no way I can do this without His help.

I must rely on His grace to make this a reality in my life. And you must too.

Let's look at our perfect example, Jesus, who stepped into His grace place and completed to the last detail what His Father assigned Him to do.

Law Meets Grace

In Luke 2:41-49 we see Jesus as a twelve year old boy going to Jerusalem with his parents to celebrate Passover. When his family left to go back to Nazareth, Jesus stayed behind in Jerusalem. When his parents searched for him in their caravan and couldn't find him, they were justifiably worried. Scripture says they searched for him for 3 days and found him in the courts of the temple conversing with the teachers or we could say Rabbis.

This passage of scripture is so full of meaning I can't help but plant here for a minute. When I get to Heaven one of the things I want to know is the details of the conversation between Jesus as a twelve year old boy and these Jewish teachers of the law. Whatever it was they were "astonished and overwhelmed with bewildered wonder."

Now I consider myself a fairly intelligent guy, but I would not go so far as to say anyone who has ever had a conversation with me walked away from it feeling astonished and overwhelmed with bewildered wonder.

And they said this of a twelve year old!!

Let's back up to verse 40 in Luke 2. It says:

"And the Child grew and became strong in spirit, filled with wisdom; and the grace (favor and spiritual blessing) of God was upon Him."

Also, in John 1:17 it says:

"For while the Law was given through Moses, grace (unearned, undeserved favor and spiritual blessing) and truth came through Jesus Christ."

My friend, Jesus is the person of Grace.

So here we have in the temple courts the law represented by the Rabbis and Grace represented by Jesus and the law was "astonished and overwhelmed with bewildered wonder."

God's grace is so amazing that when we try to understand it we are astonished and overwhelmed. It seems too good to be true that God would take our sins and put them on His beloved Son at the cross and in turn give us His righteousness. (2 Cor. 5:21) (Rom 3:21-26)

Also, I think it's interesting to point out they were sitting in the courts of the temple. The temple court was the place where everyone could come and go freely. But the holy place was reserved for the priests and the holy of holies was accessible only once a year. The holy place and the holy of holies were separated by a huge veil.

Little did those teachers of the law know they were sitting with the very person who when He gave his life on the cross would tear the veil allowing man to have direct access to God.

Jesus' mission on this earth was to reconcile the relationship between God and man and He did that by giving His life as a sacrifice for us.

When law met grace that day, the law was astonished and overwhelmed.

The law signifies man's effort to be righteous and grace is God freely giving us His righteousness.

You are not going to be able to step into your grace place by relying on your self efforts rather by relying on His grace, but we'll go deeper on that in the next chapter.

Also, it's fascinating to me to think about the Rabbis who had just celebrated Passover and were now talking with THE passover lamb – the one whose sacrifice would once and for all forgive our sins. (Hebrews 10:1-18)

Jesus Meets Opposition

Notice when his parents finally find Him, Jesus says:

> *"How is it that you had to look for Me? Did you not see and know that it is necessary [as a duty] for Me to be in My Father's house and [occupied] about My Father's business?"*

Don't let other people stop you from stepping into your grace place, especially the people who let their dreams die a long time ago.

You must be about your Father's business.

Don't let friends, family, or anyone else talk you out of what God has called you to do. Don't let the voice of naysayers get in your head.

Let negative words bounce right off of you.

Your job is too important to let someone talk you out of stepping into your grace place.

Jesus himself had people who couldn't see Him for who He really was and therefore couldn't receive from Him.

In Mark 6:1-6 it says:

> *"Jesus went away from there and came to His [own] country and hometown [Nazareth], and His disciples followed [with] Him.*
>
> *And on the Sabbath He began to teach in the synagogue; and many who listened to Him were utterly astonished, saying,*
>
> *Where did this Man acquire all this? What is the wisdom [the broad and full intelligence which has been] given to Him? What mighty works and exhibitions of power are wrought by His hands!*
>
> *Is not this the Carpenter, the son of Mary and the brother of James and Joses and Judas and Simon? And are not His sisters here among us? And they took offense at Him and were hurt [that is, they disapproved of Him, and it hindered them from acknowledging His authority] and they were caused to stumble and fall.*
>
> *But Jesus said to them, A prophet is not without honor (deference, reverence) except in his [own] country and among [his] relatives and in his [own] house.*

And He was not able to do even one work of power there, except that He laid His hands on a few sickly people [and] cured them.

And He marveled because of their unbelief (their lack of faith in Him).

And He went about among the surrounding villages and continued teaching."

They had Jesus in the flesh right there in front of them and they "disapproved of Him". Unbelievable!

So you know if the Son of God has naysayers around Him certainly you and I will.

Look at what Jesus did.

In verse 6 it says:

"He went about among the surrounding villages and continued teaching."

He continued teaching.

He didn't go home, sit in a corner, and wallow in self-pity.

It would be very discouraging to get such a cold reception from the very people who know you the best, but Jesus went right about His Father's business and continued on his mission.

Again, your grace place is too important to allow others to discourage you from it.

Keep your eyes on your Good Shepherd Jesus who will lead you right into the call He has for you.

Jesus – God's Beloved

We touched on this in the first chapter about God's love for you, but this point is so super important that it's worth repeating.

Right before Jesus steps into His ministry, he goes down to the Jordan River to be baptized by John the Baptist. As Jesus gets out of the water it says:

"the heavens were opened, and he [John] saw the Spirit of God descending like a dove and alighting on Him. And behold, a voice from heaven said, This is My Son, My Beloved, in Whom I delight!"

The King James Version says:

"This is my beloved Son, in whom I am well pleased."

This was before Jesus gave sight to the blind, cleansed the leper, fed the five thousand, and raised Lazarus from the dead. Before even Jesus performed one single miracle, we see the Father lavishing His approval on His Son.

I have the tremendous privilege of having an earthly father who loves me unconditionally. Growing up I didn't have to do anything to receive his approval.

Did I do everything right growing up? Of course not. But I never once had to be concerned my dad's love was dependent upon my good behavior. I know I am fortunate as not everyone has or had a father like mine.

But I can tell you with absolute 100% certainty your Heavenly Father loves you this way. And because He loves you you are accepted and He is well pleased with you. (Ephesians 1:6)

Jesus said in John 17:23:

"that the world may know and [definitely] recognize that You sent Me and that You have loved them [even] as You have loved Me."

And when you know you are beloved of God you can do as David said in Psalms 18:29:

"For by you I can run through a troop, and by my God I can leap over a wall."

Just as having the approval of an earthly father allows children to go through life confidently, knowing your Heavenly Father is pleased with you will cause you to have a confidence to step into your grace place no matter what may come your way.

Jesus was Dependent on the Father

We don't usually think of Jesus as being dependent on anyone for anything, but everything He did, everything He said was what He heard the Father say.

John 5:19 says:

> *"I assure you, most solemnly I tell you, the Son is able to do nothing of Himself (of His own accord); but He is able to do only what He sees the Father doing, for whatever the Father does is what the Son does in the same way [in His turn]."*

And in verse 30 of the same chapter He says:

> *"I am able to do nothing from Myself [independently, of My own accord--but only as I am taught by God and as I get His orders].*
>
> *Even as I hear, I judge [I decide as I am bidden to decide. As the voice comes to Me, so I give a decision], and My judgment is right (just, righteous), because I do not seek or consult My own will [I have no desire to do what is pleasing to Myself, My own aim, My own purpose] but only the will and pleasure of the Father Who sent Me."*

In this world being dependent on someone else is a sign of weakness. Children are dependent on their parents because they can't provide for themselves and thus society looks upon them as being weaker than adults.

But in God's Kingdom things are the opposite of the world. For example, the Bible says when you give, more will be given back to you. (Luke 6:38)

In the world's economy, when you give you have less.

The world says that to pursue our dreams we must work hard, get a good education, and work hard some more. Not that there is anything wrong with working hard and getting an education. But you must not rely on those things.

The very meaning of grace place is that it is His grace that puts you there.

It's not your self effort.

I am not saying you won't have to work, but Paul describes this beautifully in 1 Corinthians 15:10 when he says:

> *"But by the grace (the unmerited favor and blessing) of God I am what I am, and His grace toward me was not [found to be] for nothing (fruitless and without effect). In fact, I worked harder than all of them [the apostles], though it was not really I, but the grace (the unmerited favor and blessing) of God which was with me."*

God's grace produces the results.

We just need to have the posture of "God, use me. God, I'm available. God, take these dreams and desires you have placed within me and use them for your glory."

If Jesus was dependent on the Father to fulfill to the last detail the assignment He was given, how much more do you and I need to be dependent on Him?

If this chapter is making you question everything you have done in your life that's good, but please don't put yourself under condemnation if up to this point you have been living your life out of your own efforts.

I am here to encourage you and tell you Jesus is so patient and compassionate and He is ever ready to lift you up by his grace so you can step into your grace place.

Look at the beautiful story of how Jesus restored Peter.

Can you imagine how much guilt Peter must have felt after denying Jesus? He probably thought there is no way he could ever get back into the ministry.

In John 21:3 we see Peter say to some of the other disciples "I am going fishing."

It's like he's saying, "Well, I messed up so badly I am just going to go back to fishing."

But Jesus shows up after they had caught nothing and instructs them to cast their nets on the other side of the boat and they caught a huge load of fish. When they got onto the beach, Jesus was there cooking them breakfast.

I don't believe there are any insignificant details in the Bible. It says in verse 9 of John 21:

> "When they got out on land (the beach), they saw a fire of coals there and fish lying on it [cooking], and bread."

Where else does the words "fire of coals" show up in Peter's life?

In John 18 Jesus is arrested and brought before the Jewish authorities, but Peter was outside of the court and verse 18 says:

> "Now the servants and the guards (the attendants) had made a fire of coals, for it was cold, and they were standing and warming themselves. And Peter was with them, standing and warming himself."

This was the very place Peter denied Jesus.

I can imagine when Peter saw Jesus cooking breakfast on a fire of coals he would have been reminded of his denial.

It would have been a very painful thought and Jesus knew that, but I submit to you the reason the Bible makes it clear Jesus was cooking on a fire of coals was because Jesus wanted Peter to be free from that guilt and condemnation.

He then goes on to restore Peter to the ministry by instructing him to feed His sheep.

Isn't that awesome?!

My friend, no matter what you have done, Jesus is waiting for you to run to Him so He can show you His marvelous grace. It is not too late for you to step into your grace place.

All you need to do is say "Jesus, thank you for forgiving me. I will no longer rely on my own efforts. I rely on your grace to help me complete the work you have given me to do."

Jesus was Determined to Fulfill God's Mission

Let's face it. There are times when our flesh does not want to do what we know we have to do.

And this is no more evident in the life of Jesus than his conversation with the Father in the Garden of Gethsemane. In Matthew 26:39 it says Jesus:

> *"threw Himself upon the ground on His face and prayed saying, My Father, if it is possible, let this cup pass away from Me; nevertheless, not what I will [not what I desire], but as You will and desire."*

I cannot imagine what Jesus was going through at that moment. He knew what awaited Him and His flesh desperately cried out to be relieved of it. Yet, Jesus knew in order to completely fulfill to the last detail the mission God had given Him, He must go through with it.

There must be a resolve that arises within you that says "By God's grace, I'm doing this."

Jesus says in John 16:33:

> "I have told you these things, so that in Me you may have [perfect] peace and confidence. In the world you have tribulation and trials and distress and frustration; but be of good cheer [take courage; be confident, certain, undaunted]! For I have overcome the world. [I have deprived it of power to harm you and have conquered it for you.]"

Jesus promises there are trials and tribulation and frustration in this world, but to "be of good cheer" because He has "overcome the world."

You are not alone in this.

The very God who has placed these dreams, desires, talents, and abilities within you will grace you to do it.

And you know what is even more amazing?

He will also reward you for doing what He gave you the grace to do. (Hebrews 11:6)

I'm going to end this chapter where I started and that's with John 17:4:

> "I have glorified You down here on the earth by completing the work that You gave Me to do."

You can complete your assignment and by God's grace you will.

Rely on that grace and watch God do "superabundantly, far over and above all that we [dare] ask or think [infinitely beyond our highest prayers, desires, thoughts, hopes, or dreams]"

(Ephesians 3:20)

Chapter 5

How to Find Your Grace Place

1 Peter 4:10 says:

> *"As each of you has received a gift (a particular spiritual talent, a gracious divine endowment), employ it for one another as [befits] good trustees of God's many-sided grace [faithful stewards of the extremely diverse powers and gifts granted to Christians by unmerited favor]."*

It's easy to mistake the phrase grace place to simply mean your job or your career, but it's much more than these things.

Vocation is a much better word.

I love Webster's 1828 definition of vocation - "a calling by the will of God; or the bestowment of God's distinguishing grace upon a person or nation, by which that person or nation is put in the way of salvation. Summons; call; inducement."

Our English word vocation actually comes from the Latin word vocare' which means "to call."

In *48 Days to the Work you Love*, Dan Miller says "A calling is something you have to listen for, attuning yourself to the message. Vocation then is not so much pursuing a goal as it is listening for a voice." (Miller 65)

Dan goes on to explain your career is "a line of work, but never the only way to fulfill one's calling." (Miller 67)

And finally, one's job is what you do on a daily basis in order to earn money.

Let's use an example of a teacher. Usually teachers go into that profession because they love children. So a calling, vocation or grace place for a teacher could be "to educate and train children."

The career could be a school teacher, but one could also fulfill this call by working for or even volunteering for their church's kids program.

And finally, the job could be being a 4th grade teacher at South Elementary School in Pendleton, Indiana.

My mom is a great example of this. She became a teacher (career) because she loves children and wanted to educate them (grace place). However, she didn't have the same job over the whole course of her career. She taught in several public schools and one christian school and she taught different grades during her career.

Do you see the difference between grace place (calling, vocation), career, and job?

Did you know the Hebrew word for work is the same for the word worship?

It's avodah.

Dan Miller again explains it beautifully:

"To the Hebrew man, what he was doing on Thursday morning was just as much an expression of worship as being in the synagogue on the Sabbath. Nothing in scripture depicts the Christian life as divided into sacred and secular parts. Rather, it shows a unified life, one of wholeness, in which everything we do is service to God, including our daily work, whatever that may be." (Miller 68)

Colossians 3:17 says:

"And whatever you do [no matter what it is] in word or deed, do everything in the name of the Lord Jesus and in [dependence upon] His Person, giving praise to God the Father through Him."

And in verse 23 and 24 of the same chapter Paul writes:

"Whatever may be your task, work at it heartily (from the soul), as [something done] for the Lord and not for men reminding [with all certainty] that it is from the Lord [and not from men] that you will receive the inheritance which is your [real] reward. [The One Whom] you are actually serving [is] the Lord Christ (the Messiah)."

Verse 17 is key. It says:

"do everything in the name of the Lord Jesus and in dependence upon His person."

That's the very essence of your grace place. To step into your grace place, you will need to be dependent upon Him.

Now that we have differentiated between our grace place, our career, and our job, let's dig into the reason you probably grabbed this book – to find out what your grace place is.

I believe if you're at this point in the book you want for your life what Paul says in Colossians 1:10:

"That you may walk (live and conduct yourselves) in a manner worthy of the Lord, fully pleasing to Him and desiring to please Him in all things, bearing fruit in every good work and steadily growing and increasing in and by the knowledge of God [with fuller, deeper, and clearer insight, acquaintance, and recognition]."

You wouldn't even be reading this book if you didn't desire to please the Lord and to bear fruit for Him.

Allow me to let you in on a little secret here...you're already pleasing to Him.

As we discussed earlier, God sees you through His Son, Jesus. Therefore you are already beloved and accepted and pleasing in His sight. If you get a revelation of this it will set you free from striving to be pleasing to God.

Let me ask you this - does a grape have to strive to be a grape?

Further, does a grapevine have to strive to produce grapes?

What does a grapevine have to do to produce grapes? It needs to stay planted in the soil and receive water and sunshine.

Does this illustration remind you of a verse of scripture? Let's look at John 15.

John 15:1-5 (KJV) says:

> *"I am the true vine, and my Father is the husbandman.*
>
> *Every branch in me that beareth not fruit he taketh away: and every branch that beareth fruit, he purgeth it, that it may bring forth more fruit.*
>
> *Now ye are clean through the word which I have spoken unto you.*
>
> *Abide in me, and I in you. As the branch cannot bear fruit of itself, except it abide in the vine; no more can ye, except ye abide in me.*
>
> *I am the vine, ye are the branches: He that abideth in me, and I in him, the same bringeth forth much fruit: for without me ye can do nothing."*

Have you ever read this passage of scripture and thought "Oh my, I better bear fruit so God doesn't cut me off!"?

Let me share with you something about this passage that was such a relief to me when I heard it.

The Greek word for taketh away used here is *airo* which means "to lift up." You see, a grapevine needs to be up in the air to bear fruit. That is why grapevines are planted with trellises. If a grapevine is on the ground it cannot bear fruit.

Grapevines that are left on the ground are more susceptible to diseases and attack by pests than those that are supported on trellises or other off-ground structures.

(http://homeguides.sfgate.com/happens-grapevines-left-ground-66795.html)

Isn't that awesome?!

The Lord is not going to cut you off and cast you off and throw you aside if you're not bearing fruit. He is going to gently and lovingly lift you up so you can bear fruit for Him.

And in verse 2 it says every branch that bears fruit "he purgeth it". That sounds like a painful process. In the Greek however, the word is *kathairō* which means to cleanse of filth and to cleanse us from guilt. That's a whole different picture than the one we grew up believing.

This is our Jesus.

When we're feeling down and the devil is running all over us, He lifts us up so we can bear fruit and He cleanses us from all of our guilt. Wow!

To get a better revelation of this I encourage you to watch this clip from Pastor Joseph Prince
- https://www.youtube.com/watch?v=ykK70mNBGfA

Verse 3 goes on to say we are "clean through the word."

Jesus washes us through His word. Ephesians 5:26 talks about Jesus and the church when he says "having cleansed her by the washing of water with the Word."

42

The church is not a building. It's the body of Christ – you and I as believers.

So what is the point of this illustration in relation to finding your grace place?

It's this – stay connected to Jesus, abide in the vine, allow Him to wash you with His word and you can't but help but bear fruit and fulfill his call on your life.

A grapevine doesn't struggle to bear grapes and neither should you struggle to bear fruit and be in your grace place. This is the very picture of grace. You and I are the branches and we produce fruit when we abide in Jesus, our vine. A branch that is connected to the vine automatically bears fruit.

Do you see this? You are the branch. Abide in Jesus and the result will be fruit.

You might be thinking "It can't be that simple."

My friend, it is that simple.

"Surely I have to do something!!" you might say.

Yes. You do. You have to abide in the vine.

When you abide in the vine, the life blood of that vine, the sap will flow through you and produce the fruit that the world can see, touch, and taste.

"Stop being spiritual, Ryan, and tell me what I have to do practically!"

You have to listen.

As I quoted earlier in this chapter Dan Miller said "A calling is something you have to listen for, attuning yourself to the message. Vocation then is not so much pursuing a goal as it is listening for a voice." (Miller 65)

He asks in the same chapter - "How does God "call" us except through giving us talents and abilities, personality traits and passions that draw us in a particular direction?" (Miller 66)

Here are some practical questions to ask yourself that might help you through this process.

What comes natural to you?

What are you really good at?

Where would others say your talents lie?

What excites you?

What topic can you talk about for hours?

What energizes you?

If you could do anything you want in life, what would it be?

What dreams and desires have you had since you were young?

If it helps, ask people who know you really well to answer these questions. Sometimes other people can see things in us we don't see.

And most importantly, simply ask the Lord what your grace place is and how to fulfill that call throughout your daily life, but when you ask, be sure to listen.

He's already speaking to you by way of the talents, dreams, and desires He's placed within you, but if you're like me sometimes I need a little more concrete direction.

One of my favorite verses to quote when I'm needing some direction is Proverbs 16:3:

"Roll your works upon the Lord [commit and trust them wholly to Him; He will cause your thoughts to become agreeable to His will, and] so shall your plans be established and succeed."

I love the part that says "He will cause your thoughts to become agreeable to His will."

When you come to Lord and simply say "Lord, I want to fulfill your call on my life. I want to bear fruit for you the world can see. I trust you with my life and I commit all of my works to you." He promises us that He will cause our thoughts to become agreeable to His will. And when that happens we will have success.

Just come to Him.

He is there with open arms ready to hang out with you and lead you in the way in which you should go. (Isaiah 48:17)

As I'm writing this book I am asking the Holy Spirit to download to me His words. His words will change your life. My words won't have that affect.

Think of a flash drive you plug into a computer to download the files onto. In order for that flash drive to receive the files it has to be plugged in.

We need to be plugged in (abide in the vine) to Jesus so His divine life and wisdom can flow through us to reach a lost and dying world. We abide in Him by spending time with Him in prayer and seeking Him through His word.

Jesus spent a great deal of time in prayer. In Luke 6:12 it says He spent the whole night in prayer and the next morning selected His disciples.

In my own life, I cannot tell you the number of times I have received wisdom, direction, and ideas while praying.

In John 16 Jesus describes the role of the Holy Spirit. He calls him our Comforter, Counselor, Helper, Advocate, Intercessor, Strengthener, and Standby. And Jesus says that this Counselor is in "close fellowship" with us.

Remember back to your days in school when you had a test to take. Let's say it's a math test. Wouldn't it have been awesome to have a math genius sitting beside you to help you answer all the questions?

Can you imagine how much better you would have scored if that were the case?

Now imagine, having a genius sitting next to you and ignoring his help.

Don't we sometimes do this with the Holy Spirit? He is the genius in every situation we will face in life and He is eager to help us.

The secret to any success I have had in my marriage, business and every other area of life has been because of my listening to the leading of the Holy Spirit.

Have I made mistakes? Definitely.

But my goal is to lead a spirit lead life and to become more in tune to Him.

Jesus says in John 15:11:

"I have told you these things, that My joy and delight may be in you, and that your joy and gladness may be of full measure and complete and overflowing."

When you are connected to Jesus and abiding in Him, you will bear fruit and be in your grace place. And that is the place in your life where your joy and gladness will be of "full measure and complete and overflowing."

Dan Miller says:

"When there is an alignment of our skills, abilities, talents, personality traits, and passions, we will recognize God's "call."

We will have found our sweet spot and will experience work that is fulfilling, meaningful, purposeful, and profitable." (Miller 66)

Chapter 6

The Example of Joseph

The life of Joseph is so rich in stories that we can learn from and apply to our own life.

Let's dig into his life and pull out the nuggets.

Genesis 37 begins his story that goes on for a total of 14 chapters. The book of Genesis is 50 chapters long so 28% of the whole book is dedicated to the life of Joseph.

Do you reckon God is trying to tell us something here?

The number 14 in Hebrew means "deliverance" and that word sums up Joseph's life. He delivered his family from starvation and had them dwell in the land of Goshen which means "drawing near."

In Genesis 45:10 Joseph says:

"You will live in the land of Goshen, and you will be close to me-- you and your children and your grandchildren, your flocks, your herds, and all you have."

Our provision is close to our shepherd, Jesus. It's His responsibility to feed us, guide us, and shield us.

Psalms 23 says:

"THE LORD is my Shepherd [to feed, guide, and shield me], I shall not lack."

So let's go back to Genesis 37 where the story of Joseph begins and see what we can glean from his life that will help us in fulfilling the call God has on our life.

Verse 5 says:

> *"Now Joseph had a dream and he told it to his brothers, and they hated him still more."*

Now Joseph' brothers already didn't like him because his father loved him more than his other brothers.

We should go through life acting as if we are God's favorite child. I know He doesn't love us more than all of His other children, but if we can grow in our revelation of God's love for us, that will empower us and give us a confidence that others won't have.

In chapter 37 Joseph was very young – about 17 years old when he was sold into slavery by his brothers. A 17 year old boy doesn't have the maturity of an older man and we see that when Joseph tells his brothers his dreams about them bowing down to him. Jacob, his father, had the proper response when in verse 11 it says "he pondered over it."

This word "pondered" reminds me of Luke 2:19 when the shepherds told Mary about their visitation from the angel who told them about the Messiah being born:

> *"But Mary was keeping within herself all these things (sayings), weighing and pondering them in her heart."*

You might have some extravagant dreams and desires for your life which have been placed there by the Lord. I caution you to use wisdom in who you tell those dreams to. Not everyone is going to "get it."

Instead, ponder over them in your heart and let Him bring them to pass in His timing.

Also, be aware that once you start moving in the direction of your grace place, not everyone is going to be your cheerleader.

You may have friends or family that turn out to not be so supportive.

Do not let that stop you from pursuing what is in your heart.

Your mission is too important to let naysayers talk you out of what you know you're supposed to do.

Joseph's brothers actually wanted to kill him, but instead they sold him to some Ishmaelite merchants passing by for twenty pieces of silver, who took him captive and brought him to Egypt He was sold to Potiphar who was an "officer of Pharaoh and the captain and chief executioner of the royal guard". (Genesis 37:36)

Genesis 39:2-6 are some of my favorite verses in this story:

> "But the Lord was with Joseph, and he [though a slave] was a successful and prosperous man; and he was in the house of his master the Egyptian. And his master saw that the Lord was with him and that the Lord made all that he did to flourish and succeed in his hand. So Joseph pleased [Potiphar] and found favor in his sight, and he served him. And [his master] made him supervisor over his house and he put all that he had in his charge.
>
> From the time that he made him supervisor in his house and over all that he had, the Lord blessed the Egyptian's house for Joseph's sake; and the Lord's blessing was on all that he had in the house and in the field.
>
> And [Potiphar] left all that he had in Joseph's charge and paid no attention to anything he had except the food he ate."

I have often wondered why Joseph had so much favor. Did he do anything for verse 2 to say that the Lord was with him?

Was he special?

I believe the answer is found when we study the robe which his father made for him. Verse 3 says his father made him a "[distinctive] long tunic with sleeves" or as the King James version says "a coat of many colours."

What's so special about a robe? Well, where else do we see a robe mentioned in the Bible?

One of my absolute favorite passages of scripture is the story of the Prodigal Son in Luke 15. Here it is in its entirety:

And He said, There was a certain man who had two sons;

And the younger of them said to his father, Father, give me the part of the property that falls [to me]. And he divided the estate between them.

And not many days after that, the younger son gathered up all that he had and journeyed into a distant country, and there he wasted his fortune in reckless and loose [from restraint] living.

And when he had spent all he had, a mighty famine came upon that country, and he began to fall behind and be in want.

So he went and forced (glued) himself upon one of the citizens of that country, who sent him into his fields to feed hogs.

And he would gladly have fed on and filled his belly with the carob pods that the hogs were eating, but [they could not satisfy his hunger and] nobody gave him anything [better].

Then when he came to himself, he said, How many hired servants of my father have enough food, and [even food] to spare, but I am perishing (dying) here of hunger!

I will get up and go to my father, and I will say to him, Father, I have sinned against heaven and in your sight.

I am no longer worthy to be called your son; [just] make me like one of your hired servants.

So he got up and came to his [own] father. But while he was still a long way off, his father saw him and was moved with pity and tenderness [for him]; and he ran and embraced him and kissed him [fervently].

And the son said to him, Father, I have sinned against heaven and in your sight; I am no longer worthy to be called your son [I no longer deserve to be recognized as a son of yours]!

But the father said to his bond servants, Bring quickly the best robe (the festive robe of honor) and put it on him; and give him a ring for his hand and sandals for his feet.

And bring out that [wheat-]fattened calf and kill it; and let us revel and feast and be happy and make merry,

Because this my son was dead and is alive again; he was lost and is found!

And they began to revel and feast and make merry.

But his older son was in the field; and as he returned and came near the house, he heard music and dancing.

And having called one of the servant [boys] to him, he began to ask what this meant.

And he said to him, Your brother has come, and your father has killed that [wheat-]fattened calf, because he has received him back safe and well.

But [the elder brother] was angry [with deep-seated wrath] and resolved not to go in. Then his father came out and began to plead with him,

But he answered his father, Look! These many years I have served you, and I have never disobeyed your command. Yet you never gave me [so much as] a [little] kid, that I might revel and feast and be happy and make merry with my friends;

But when this son of yours arrived, who has devoured your estate with immoral women, you have killed for him that [wheat-] fattened calf!

And the father said to him, Son, you are always with me, and all that is mine is yours.

But it was fitting to make merry, to revel and feast and rejoice, for this brother of yours was dead and is alive again!

He was lost and is found!"

Isn't this a beautiful story?

Jesus told this to reveal to us the heart of our Heavenly Father. I encourage you to read and re-read this and let it sink deep into your spirit. I know I have said this many times before in this book, but it's worth repeating –

Your Heavenly Father loves you so much!!

There is absolutely nothing you have done or could ever do to keep Him from loving you. In verse 20 the father sees his son a long way off and runs to him.

My friend, if you've been a long way off from Him, He is just waiting for you to come back to Him so He can run to you and lavish you with His love.

Allow me let you in on a little secret here – one of the devil's main attacks on people is to keep them from coming to God. He does that by giving them thoughts that God is mad at them and is looking to punish them for their mistakes.

When you believe the lie that God is mad at you, why would you ever come to Him? If you had the mafia on your tail looking to hurt you for some reason, would you show your face to them? Of course not. You would run as fast as you could and hide.

So many people today, even Christians, have the false belief God is upset with them and is looking to punish them.

Do not believe that lie!

Jesus was punished for us so we can live free of condemnation and come to our Father knowing He loves us and sees us as righteous.

So no matter what you're dealing with – come to Him. He is a loving Father and He's looking for you in the distance so He can run to you.

Verse 22 says the father requested to his servants to bring the "best robe" and put it on his son. When the prodigal son was hanging out with the hogs he devised a speech to tell his father which included the words "I am no longer worthy to be called your son."

Instead, the father put the best robe on his son along with a ring on his hand and sandals on his feet. There is so much here that a whole book could be written about it, but the significance of the robe, the ring, and the sandals are that by bestowing this honor on his son, the father is distinguishing his son from the servants.

He is in essence saying "I don't care what you have done. You are my son and you are righteous in my eyes." It was a robe of righteousness.

Isaiah 61:10 says:

> "I will greatly rejoice in the Lord, my soul will exult in my God; for He has clothed me with the garments of salvation, He has covered me with the robe of righteousness, as a bridegroom decks himself with a garland, and as a bride adorns herself with her jewels."

When you believe you are righteous you can come to your daddy God unashamed. And when you take your place as sons and daughters of God you can freely receive His blessings and reign in life (Romans 5:17)

Romans 8:15 says:

> "For [the Spirit which] you have now received [is] not a spirit of slavery to put you once more in bondage to fear, but you have received the Spirit of adoption [the Spirit producing sonship] in [the bliss of] which we cry, Abba (Father)! Father!"

The word Abba means "Daddy" or "Papa." It denotes a deep level of intimacy.

See God as your Daddy who loves you deeply and wants to pour out His blessings and favor on you and like Joseph, you will see His favor on you and everything you do will prosper. (Psalm 1)

As we continue with the life of Joseph, we see where he is falsely accused and is thrown into prison, but even in prison he had favor.

Genesis 39:21 says:

> *"But the Lord was with Joseph, and showed him mercy and loving-kindness and gave him favor in the sight of the warden of the prison."*

The Bible doesn't state exactly how long Joseph was in prison, but it was at least two years because Chapter 41 starts off by saying "After two full years..." But we don't know how long before that two years Joseph was there.

Can you imagine being in prison for something you didn't do for two years or longer?

If I was Joseph I might have been thinking those dreams God gave me were dead. How could they possibly come to pass now?

But let me tell you, friend, if those dreams and desires are from the Lord, He will bring them to pass.

The Lord knew Joseph was going to spend time in prison. Likewise, he knows your future and is already there making a way for your dreams to come true.

You may be in "prison" right now - the "prison" of waiting for those dreams and desires to come to pass.

Your job in this season is in Psalms 37:3-5:

> *"Trust (lean on, rely on, and be confident) in the Lord and do good;*
> *so shall you dwell in the land and feed surely on His faithfulness,*
> *and truly you shall be fed. Delight yourself in the Lord, and He will*
> *give you the desires and secret petitions of your heart. Commit your*
> *way to the Lord (roll and repose each care of your load on Him);*
> *trust (lean on, rely on, and be confident) also in Him and He will*
> *bring it to pass."*

So your job is to trust Him and do good.

Let's make this practical.

Let's say you really feel called to be a pastor. The unwise thing to do would be to go to your current pastor and say "Move over, buddy. God has called me to be a pastor and I'm taking over."

No. While you're waiting for that desire to come to pass go do something.

Get involved in your local church. Serve. Clean the toilets. Be an usher. Be a greeter at the door.

Do something. Don't just sit there and complain that you're not where you know God is calling you to. Be of service to your pastor.

Believe me, when you are faithful in that role, God will reward you and exalt you to the position He has in store for you. Do not exalt yourself.

Proverbs 18:16 says:

> *"A man's gift makes room for him and brings him before great*
> *men."*

Allow the Lord to bring it to pass. When he does it, it's so much better.

I know the waiting can be hard. But the time is going to pass no matter whether you're happy or complaining. Choose to be happy and trust the Lord.

As we all know, Joseph's dreams at the young age of 17 eventually came to pass. Genesis 42:6 says:

"Joseph's brothers came and bowed themselves before him with their faces to the ground."

22 years had passed from the time Joseph was sold into slavery and that moment.

You might not have to wait 22 years for your dreams and desires to come to pass, but no matter how long it is continue to trust in His faithfulness, His goodness, and He will surely bring it to pass for you.

Chapter 7

Effortless

"You make it seem effortless."

These were the words a business colleague said to me one day and he probably had no idea it was the best compliment I had ever received in regard to my business.

He was referring to how I seem to handle so many projects at one time.

Do I work hard? Yes. Absolutely.

But most of the time it doesn't feel like hard work. In fact a lot of times it's hard to distinguish between work and play. I know that might seem hard to believe, but when you're in your zone of your grace place the two get confused.

For example, some of my business partners and I just hosted a conference for e-commerce sellers a few weeks ago from the time of this writing.

Was that work? Yes. Was it fun? Yes.

For me it felt more fun than work.

Why?

The answer I believe is found in 1 Corinthians 15:10:

> *"But by the grace (the unmerited favor and blessing) of God I am what I am, and His grace toward me was not [found to be] for nothing (fruitless and without effect). In fact, I worked harder than all of them [the apostles], though it was not really I, but the grace (the unmerited favor and blessing) of God which was with me."*

It was the grace of God working through me and I was in my grace zone. When you're doing something you're good at and you're graced for, it's fun.

In contrast, when you're not good at something it's no fun at all.

When I was 8 years old, I played baseball in a local league. Baseball was not my sport. I wasn't horrible, but I definitely could not have been described as a good baseball player. Therefore, baseball was never fun for me.

Basketball on the other hand was a different story. I loved to play basketball and I was no Larry Bird, but I was pretty good. In high school I managed to score over 1200 points in my 4 years. Basketball was fun because I had some success with it.

One job I absolutely hate doing is hanging pictures. If you're a handyman that statement might sound ridiculous. If it's a very light piece of art or something that only requires one nail it's a piece of cake, but if there are two hooks on the back (one on either side) and I have to make sure I put the nails in the wall in the exact spot so that it's straight, I can get very frustrated very quickly.

However, if you tell me to get up in front of a hundred people and talk to them about how to start a business online, I'm excited.

I know. I'm odd.

But, my talents and abilities are nowhere near the handyman profession. It's almost like as soon as I pick up a hammer or other tool something inside of me cringes and is telling me "This is not where your grace lies. Hire someone to do this and go back to writing your book."

Jesus experienced this same thing in John 4 when he made a detour to Samaria to meet with the woman at the well.

In verse 4 it says:

"It was necessary for Him to go through Samaria."

Jesus was in Judea and heading north to Galilee. Normally Jewish travelers making this trip would go around Samaria to avoid contact with the Samaritans, but Jesus had a divine appointment with this woman so he went directly through Samaria.

When you are in your grace place, you are trusting in Him to lead you and guide you. He will perform in and through you. Your life is one of resting in Him and allowing Him to work through you to produce the fruit.

Now this doesn't mean you don't have to work. It means your work is Spirit led and you're trusting in Him to produce the results you could never have done by relying on your own self effort.

You give to Him your little and He multiplies it just like He did with the five loaves of bread and two pieces of fish when He fed the five thousand. (Matthew 14:13-21)

His favor on you will put you at the right place at the right time.

I have experienced this numerous times over my life. Job openings, business partnerships, even the beginning of my relationship with my wife were the result of God putting me at the right place at the right time.

I could never have done that on my own.

Proverbs 3:5-6 says:

"Lean on, trust in, and be confident in the Lord with all your heart and mind and do not rely on your own insight or understanding.

In all your ways know, recognize, and acknowledge Him, and He will direct and make straight and plain your paths."

He is your good shepherd and loves you so very much. You can trust Him to lead you in the right direction and put you exactly where you need to be at the exact right time.

Other than the fact that Jesus loves me, do you want to know what I think the secret is as to why I see so much favor in my life? I expect to see it. You might think that sounds presumptuous, but it's something God has promised me and He has promised you.

In Psalms 5:12 it says:

"For You, Lord, will bless the [uncompromisingly] righteous [him who is upright and in right standing with You]; as with a shield You will surround him with goodwill (pleasure and favor)."

Now I know some people read this verse and automatically disqualify themselves because it says the Lord will bless the righteous. And like me, you probably can probably remember some mistakes you have made. Maybe you even made one today.

But guess what, your righteousness is not about you.

If we were living in the Old Testament then that would absolutely be the case.

One's righteousness was based on keeping the law.

But I have some good news for you.

We're living under the dispensation of grace because Jesus died to the law for us and rose again for us. (Romans 7:4) (Romans 6:14)

Jesus is our righteousness. (1 Corinthians 1:30)

That means you qualify for every blessing, every favor – not because of what you have done or haven't done, but because of what Jesus did for you.

The blood of Jesus has qualified you.

See yourself as God sees you, which is righteous (2 Corinthians 5:21) and expect to be surrounded with His favor.

I made a detour there, but let's go back to Jesus and the Samaritan woman in John 4. He sits down at the well and has a conversation with this woman and ministers grace and love to her. What I want to point out is that in verse 31 his disciples come back from buying food and urge him to eat something. Jesus responds in verse 32 by saying:

> "I have food (nourishment) to eat of which you know nothing and have no idea."

Ministering to this precious woman energized Jesus.

That's what I'm talking about when I say that when you're in your grace place you will feel refreshed and energized.

It's not because you're so strong in and of yourself.

It's because you're flowing in the grace the Lord gave you and like Paul in 1 Corinthians 15:10, the grace is doing the work.

That's what I mean when I say it's effortless.

Do you think Jesus just made a detour through Samaria because they served the best hamburgers and He was hungry?

No. He was lead by the Spirit.

Did He have to walk there? Yes.

Did He have to sit down at the well? Yes.

Did He have to open His mouth and begin speaking to the woman? Yes.

My point is effortless doesn't mean no effort is involved on our part. It means you're not trusting in your efforts to produce the result.

If you have a job interview, commit it to the Lord (Proverbs 16:3), do what you need to do to prepare for it, but go to the interview trusting He will give you the words to say. Trust that His Favor will surround you. Rest in Him knowing He will take good care of you and lead you to good success.

Remember this...

Self effort = Struggle

Relying on His Grace = Restful

Back to my example of not being a handyman - If I wanted to I could start a handyman business. I know a lot about online marketing so I could use that to my advantage to get jobs. But I would loathe every minute of it. My life would be one of frustration because I wouldn't be operating in my grace place.

Maybe this describes you. If it does, please take this chapter in the spirit in which I intend it to be, which is to encourage you, not to beat you over the head.

God's grace and favor for every area of your life is available to you. All you have to do is receive it.

You might be saying "Ryan, I know what my grace place is, but I don't know how to get there."

One of my business partners is famous for saying "Nothing to it, but to do it."

Just get started.

What I mean is if you're called to serve in the nursery at your church then don't wait around and hope they ask you to help. Go to the leaders and say you would like to serve in the nursery. As a leader in my church, I can tell you that churches are always looking for faithful people to step up.

If you feel like you're called to write a book then start writing. Don't succumb to analysis paralysis. Take some action.

I promise you that if you're truly called, God will open the doors for you. You don't have to have everything figured out in advance. Just get started and He'll pave the way for you.

However, please don't be like Joseph in the Bible when he told his brothers he had received dreams from the Lord that one day his brothers would bow down to him. His dream did come true, but telling them got him into a lot of trouble and didn't endear him to his brothers.

The Lord might be giving you some very big dreams for your life. Not everyone is in a position to hear it so be wise about who you tell those dreams to. Trust the Lord and He will bring those dreams to pass in your life.

My friend, Jesus paid a high price for us to have a life that is overflowing with joy, gladness, and completeness.

When you step into what God has called you to do and you're relying on His grace, you can't help but to experience that and change the world around you by His grace which is flowing through you.

Others will describe your life as effortless and you'll just smile and say "It's the Grace of God."

Chapter 8

One Thing is Needful

You're probably familiar with the story of Mary and Martha.

Luke 10:38-42 records a time when Jesus stopped at Martha's house:

"Now while they were on their way, it occurred that Jesus entered a certain village, and a woman named Martha received and welcomed Him into her house.

And she had a sister named Mary, who seated herself at the Lord's feet and was listening to His teaching.

But Martha [overly occupied and too busy] was distracted with much serving; and she came up to Him and said, Lord, is it nothing to You that my sister has left me to serve alone? Tell her then to help me [to lend a hand and do her part along with me]!

But the Lord replied to her by saying, Martha, Martha, you are anxious and troubled about many things;

There is need of only one or but a few things. Mary has chosen the good portion [that which is to her advantage], which shall not be taken away from her."

The King James version of verse 42 says "But one thing is needful."

In this passage we see two different approaches to walking in our grace place.

I don't doubt Martha's heart was in the right place in wanting to serve the Lord. If Jesus came to my house, I would for sure want to serve him the best of what I had. I would want our house to be picked up and spotless. In the same way, when we are doing what God has called us to do, we want to do it with excellence. There's nothing wrong with that.

But we should never get so busy with our serving that we fail to do what gives us the strength to serve in the first place, which is sitting at His feet.

It is so easy to be like Martha and get distracted with how much we have to do. There will always be things to do. Life is busy and the demands placed on us don't ever seem to go away.

But all these things even if they are things you're doing for the Lord are distractions if you're neglecting the one thing – sitting at His feet.

My friend, you must take time to draw from Him.

If you want your service for Him to be effective, receive His divine life and allow that to be the strength from which you serve. If you're trying to fulfill His call on your life with your own strength, you'll end up frustrated.

Martha's focus was on what she must *do* for Jesus. Mary's focus was on Jesus himself.

When your focus is on your "do" then you become "anxious and troubled" because you can never do enough.

Your best is not enough.

There will always be more that needs to be accomplished.

There will never be enough time to get it all done. That is if your focus is on what you can do.

However, when you realize you can do nothing without Him (John 15:5) your focus is on Him and receiving from that divine life. When you receive from Him, you are empowered to go and do.

Your "do" then is from His strength within you (Philippians 4:13) and the results you get will be the God kind of results.

Your "do" will be out of the overflow of what you receive from Him.

Think of a television. In order for it to work it must 1) Be plugged into a power source and 2) Be connected to either an antenna, a DVR, a cable box, or if you have a smart TV, the internet. The television itself does not have the ability to show programming unless it first receives it from somewhere.

In the same way, we can't hope to completely fulfill the call of God on our life if we're not abiding in the Vine and allowing His divine life to flow through us and produce the fruit. If we haven't first received from Him, we don't have anything to give those around us.

Another appropriate example is a cell phone. What happens to your phone when you use it continually? The battery loses power and eventually it will completely be depleted and you can't use your phone until you plug it back in and recharge it.

We're much the same way. I notice in my own life that if I go a day or two without spending some time with the Lord in His word and in prayer, I feel worn down. We are refreshed in His presence when we're sitting at His feet.

Psalm 23:3 says:

"He refreshes and restores my life (my self)"

But do you want to know the advantage we have over every single person that lived before the cross? We as believers have the Holy Spirit of God living inside of us. In the Old Testament the Holy Spirit just came *upon* people and then left. As a result of what Jesus did for us we have the Holy Spirit living *inside* us.

In John 16:7 Jesus says:

"However, I am telling you nothing but the truth when I say it is profitable (good, expedient, advantageous) for you that I go away.

Because if I do not go away, the Comforter (Counselor, Helper, Advocate, Intercessor, Strengthener, Standby) will not come to you [into close fellowship with you];but if I go away, I will send Him to you [to be in close fellowship with you]."

Jesus had to preface this verse by saying "I am telling you nothing but the truth."

It's hard to imagine having a better situation than to be able to walk and talk with Jesus in the flesh.

But think about it this way. If Jesus were alive on the earth today and lived in Israel, we would have to physically get on a plane to go see Him. Then we would never want to leave and Israel would become overcrowded with people.

Can you imagine the long lines there would be to get a chance to meet Him?

There are over 7 billion people in the world today. I know not all of them would be able to make the trip, but it would be like Disney World in the summer time.

I know that's a little silly to think about, but because we have the Holy Spirit, we are never away from God. We have it so much better than the disciples did than when Jesus physically walked the earth.

When they had a need they had to go get Jesus. When we have a need, it's as simple as crying out to Him.

There's a song I like from Bethel called "Come to Me." The first part of the song says:

"I am the Lord your God, I go before you now
I stand beside you, I'm all around you
Though you feel I'm far away, I'm closer than your breath
I am with you, more than you know"

My friend, all you need to do is simply come to Him to receive the refreshing for your soul.

Because we have the awesome benefit of the Holy Spirit in our lives there is also another huge advantage we have over the saints in the Old Testament and that is the Holy Spirit will partner up with us in prayer. Jesus called him the "Intercessor" as we saw in John 16:7.

Do you want to know the absolute best way to build up and refresh yourself?

It's by praying in the Holy Spirit or as is many times called praying in tongues.

Now before you get all upset and throw this book down if you're reading a hard copy or smash your Kindle if you're reading the ebook version, let me show you the word of God on it.

I Corinthians 14:2 says:

> *"For one who speaks in an [unknown] tongue speaks not to men but to God, for no one understands or catches his meaning, because in the [Holy] Spirit he utters secret truths and hidden things [not obvious to the understanding]."*

1 Corinthians 14:14,15 says:

> *"For if I pray in an [unknown] tongue, my spirit [by the Holy Spirit within me] prays, but my mind is unproductive [it bears no fruit and helps nobody].*
>
> *Then what am I to do? I will pray with my spirit [by the Holy Spirit that is within me], but I will also pray [intelligently] with my mind*

and understanding; I will sing with my spirit [by the Holy Spirit that is within me], but I will sing [intelligently] with my mind and understanding also."

And in Verse 18 of the same chapter Paul says:

"I thank God that I speak in [strange] tongues (languages) more than any of you or all of you put together."

And in verse 39 of the same chapter Paul says:"and do not forbid or hinder speaking in [unknown] tongues."

Now let me say what I'm referring to here is not the gift of tongues as mentioned in 1 Corinthians 12:10 where there must be an interpretation. I'm talking about a personal prayer language every believer can receive and it's what Paul is talking about when he says "praying in the spirit."

I understand you might have been raised to believe tongues is not for the church today. The church I grew up in for the first 12 years of my life didn't believe in tongues either so I get it.

But please please don't let tradition supersede the Word of God on this. Study it out for yourself.

No matter where you come out on the subject please know you are loved and accepted by Him. Please hear my heart on this. I have friends that believe completely different than me on this subject, but that in no way hinders our relationship. We are all brothers and sisters in the Lord. There is way too much we have in common to let a few disagreements hinder us from being united from our main purpose which is to preach the good news of Jesus Christ.

But I would be doing you a disservice if I didn't tell you about the impact praying in the Spirit has had on my life.

With absolute certainty I can say I would not be where I am today without spending time praying in the Spirit. There are times in my life when I have a problem I don't know what to do about or simply don't know how to pray about it. In Romans 8:26 it says:

"So too the [Holy] Spirit comes to our aid and bears us up in our weakness; for we do not know what prayer to offer nor how to offer it worthily as we ought, but the Spirit Himself goes to meet our supplication and pleads in our behalf with unspeakable yearnings and groanings too deep for utterance."

I have received ideas for my business as a result of time spent praying in the Spirit. This book is a result of that time as well.

But maybe even more important than all of that is time spent praying in the Spirit builds us up.

Jude 20 says:

"But you, beloved, build yourselves up [founded] on your most holy faith [make progress, rise like an edifice higher and higher], praying in the Holy Spirit;"

I don't know about you, but I can use all the building up I can get.

With all of that being said, the purpose of this book is not to break down every scripture on the subject of praying in the Spirit so if you would like to learn more about the Holy Spirit here are some resources I recommend:

The God I Never Knew: How Real Friendship with the Holy Spirit Can Change Your Life by Pastor Robert Morris

The God I Never Knew Sermon Series by Pastor Robert Morris

Tongues – Our God Given Gift by Pastor Joseph Prince

The Baptism of the Holy Spirit by Joyce Meyer

So again, please know no matter where you come out on this subject I love you.

Whether you choose to spend time at Jesus' feet by reading the word, praying in English or by praying in the Spirit the important thing is to take the time to receive from Him to get the refreshing your soul needs to effectively walk in your grace place.

Chapter 9

Take Action

You're at the end of this book, but not at the end of your journey of walking in your grace place.

Whenever I read a new book or purchase a new education course, I'm asking myself questions like "What does this mean for me?", "How can I apply this to my life?", and "What is the next action I need to take to implement this?"

I encourage you to ask yourself these questions too.

What is your next action?

I will consider this book a success if you simply realize just how much God loves you, how righteous you are in Christ, and how qualified you are. Because if you can get a revelation of those things, you can't but help to reign in life. (Romans 5:17)

So here's your homework:

- Read and re-read the chapters in this book about how much God loves you and has qualified you.

- Listen to Jesus-filled sermons that impart grace.

- Meditate on scriptures that speak of His love for you and your righteousness in Christ.

- Spend time praying about where your grace place is. The Lord is faithful and will show you where it is you will flourish.

- If you already know where your grace place is, take steps in that direction.

- Whatever you "do", do it trusting and relying on Him and His grace.

My prayer for you is what Jesus prayed in John 17:4:

"I glorified you on earth by completing down to the last detail what you assigned me to do."

In and of ourselves this is an impossible task, but you now know you can't rely on your own efforts. Paul says in 1 Corinthians 15:10:

"But by the grace (the unmerited favor and blessing) of God I am what I am, and His grace toward me was not [found to be] for nothing (fruitless and without effect). In fact, I worked harder than all of them [the apostles], though it was not really I, but the grace (the unmerited favor and blessing) of God which was with me."

His grace is sufficient for you and will produce the desired results. It's our job to abide in Him, sit at His feet, and let His divine life flow through us to reach the world around us.

My friend, your part in all of this is crucial. It's a part I can't play. You have a special God given gift people need.

I encourage you to seek the Lord to find out what your part is and when you find it, to step into it with your whole heart.

You can do it.

You must do it.

There is a world out there that is desperate for that talent you have.

Let's do this.

Dear Friend,

I'm honored you took the time to read this book. It's a message that has been on my heart for quite some time.

I truly believe if enough believers can figure out what it is they're called to do and actually do it that we can change the world.

My hope and prayer is you realize that your place of grace is not a demand you must do, but that God is there supplying the grace we need to step into our grace place.

Could you do me a huge favor? If this book has blessed you please email me and let me know. My personal email is ryan@findingyourgraceplace.com. I do my best to respond personally to all messages I receive. Also, you can find me on Facebook at https://www.facebook.com/ryanreger/

I love you and thank you for taking your precious time to read what has been on my heart.

By His Grace,

Study Guide

Over the next few pages are some take aways and questions to ponder from each chapter. Please take the time to review the key points from each chapter and to ask yourself the questions. There is some space between each question to write your responses.

Chapter 1
Jesus Loves You

Take Aways

The key to becoming convinced of His love is to meditate on scriptures that talk about His love for you.

When you know the love God has for you, you can conquer any challenge life throws at you.

When you know God loves you, you know He is for you. And when you know He is for you, you know there is no devil in hell that can stop you from fulfilling His call on your life and you walking in your grace place.

You are so dearly loved by our Heavenly Father.

Questions to Ponder

Do I have a revelation of God's Love for me?

What are some scriptures I can meditate on about God's love?

Chapter 2
What is a Grace Place?

Take Aways

Grace is the free and undeserved favor and love of God.

Just as you were saved by the grace of God, that same grace can flow to every area of your life and in order to be effective for Him in those areas you desperately need His grace.

Your grace place is the reason you were created, your calling.

Your gifts, talents, and abilities point to your grace place and give you a clue as to what yours might be.

The main point I want to emphasize throughout this whole book is to completely fulfill the calling God has for you you're going to have to completely rely on Him.

Grace produces the empowerment to do what you could not do on your own.

His grace working through you will produce the God kind of results.

Questions to Ponder

What are you really good at?

What comes natural to you?

Are there desires in your heart that have been there since you were young that you have yet to accomplish?

What is it for you that energizes you?

What topic can you talk about for hours?

Chapter 3
He has Qualified You

Takeaways

To fully step into your grace place, your focus has to be on Him, on His love for you, on His grace.

Here is the truth about you:

You are qualified. Colossians 1:12 says:

> *"Who has qualified and made us fit"*

You are the righteousness of God in Christ. Romans 5:21 says:

> *"For our sake He made Christ [virtually] to be sin Who knew no sin, so that in and through Him we might become [endued with, viewed as being in, and examples of] the righteousness of God [what we ought to be, approved and acceptable and in right relationship with Him, by His goodness]."*

You are completely forgiven. Psalm 103:12 says:

> *"As far as the east is from the west, so far has He removed our transgressions from us."*

Romans 8:1:

> *"There is therefore now no condemnation to them which are in Christ Jesus"*

There is nothing you have done in your past that can disqualify you from stepping into your grace place.

Questions to Ponder

Have I let a past mistake stop me from moving forward into God's call for my life?

What am I going to do different to no longer let my past hold me back?

Chapter 4
Jesus – Our Perfect Example

Takeaways

John 17:4 says:

> *"I have glorified You down here on the earth by completing the work that You gave Me to do."*

Jesus is the person of Grace.

The law signifies man's effort to be righteous and grace is God freely giving us His righteousness.

Don't let other people stop you from stepping into your grace place, especially the people who let their dreams die a long time ago.

Keep your eyes on your Good Shepherd Jesus who will lead you right into the call He has for you.

Just as having the approval of an earthly father allows children to go through life confidently, knowing your Heavenly Father is pleased with you will cause you to have a confidence to step into your grace place no matter what may come your way.

We just need to have the posture of "God, use me. God, I'm available.

God, take these dreams and desires you have placed within me and use them for your glory."

My friend, no matter what you have done, Jesus is waiting for you to run to Him so He can show you His marvelous grace. It is not too late for you to step into your grace place.

The very God who has placed these dreams, desires, talents, and abilities within you will grace you to do it.

Questions to Ponder

If you have negative people in your life who don't understand your dreams and desires what can you do to not let that stop you?

What is your relationship with your earthly father like? Has that helped/hindered your relationship with your Heavenly father?

Chapter 5
How to Find Your Grace Place

Takeaways

Allow me to let you in on a little secret here...you're already pleasing to Him.

When we're feeling down and the devil is running all over us, He lifts us up so we can bear fruit and He cleanses us from all of our guilt.

Stay connected to Jesus, abide in the vine, allow Him to wash you with His word and you can't but help but bear fruit and fulfill his call on your life.

A grapevine doesn't struggle to bear grapes and neither should you struggle to bear fruit and be in your grace place. This is the very picture of grace. You and I are the branches and we produce fruit when we abide in Jesus, our vine. A branch that is connected to the vine automatically bears fruit.

"How does God "call" us except through giving us talents and abilities, personality traits and passions that draw us in a particular direction?"

Just come to Him.

We need to be plugged in (abide in the vine) to Jesus so His divine life and wisdom can flow through us to reach a lost and dying world. We abide in Him by spending time with Him in prayer and seeking Him through His word.

When you are connected to Jesus and abiding in Him, you will bear fruit and be in your grace place. And that is the place in your life where your joy and gladness will be of "full measure and complete and overflowing."

Questions to Ponder

What comes natural to you?

What are you really good at?

Where would others say your talents lie?

What excites you?

What topic can you talk about for hours?

What energizes you?

If you could do anything you want in life, what would it be?

What dreams and desires have you had since you were young?

Chapter 6
The Example of Joseph

Takeaways

We should go through life acting as if we are God's favorite child. I know He doesn't love us more than all of His other children, but if we can grow in our revelation of God's love for us, that will empower us and give us a confidence others won't have.

You might have some extravagant dreams and desires for your life that have been placed there by the Lord. I caution you to use wisdom in who you tell those dreams to. Not everyone is going to "get it."

There is absolutely nothing you have done or could ever do to keep Him from loving you.

If you've been a long way off from Him, He is just waiting for you to come back to Him so He can run to you and lavish you with His love.

Jesus was punished for us so we can live free of condemnation and come to our Father knowing He loves us and sees us as righteous.

So no matter what you're dealing with – come to Him. He is a loving Father and He's looking for you in the distance so He can run to you.

See God as your Daddy who loves you deeply and wants to pour out His blessings and favor on you and like Joseph, you will see His favor on you and everything you do will prosper.

You might not have to wait 22 years for your dreams and desires to come to pass, but no matter how long it is continue to trust in His faithfulness, His goodness, and He will surely bring it to pass for you.

Questions to Ponder

Do you see God as a loving Father or a harsh judge?

Are you reluctant to come to Him?

What scriptures can you meditate on to get a revelation of his goodness and heart of love toward you?

Chapter 7
Effortless

Takeaways

When you're doing something you're good at and you're graced for, it's fun.

When you are in your grace place, you are trusting in Him to lead you and guide you. He will perform in and through you. Your life is one of resting in Him and allowing Him to work through you to produce the fruit. Now this doesn't mean you don't have to work. It means your work is Spirit led and you're trusting in Him to produce the results you could never have done by relying on your own self effort.

His favor on you will put you at the right place at the right time.

He is your good shepherd and loves you so very much. You can trust Him to lead you in the right direction and put you exactly where you need to be at the exact right time.

That means you qualify for every blessing, every favor – not because of what you have done or haven't done, but because of what Jesus did for you.

That's what I'm talking about when I say when you're in your grace place you will feel refreshed and energized.

My point is effortless doesn't mean no effort is involved on our part. It means you're not trusting in your efforts to produce the result.

Self effort = Struggle

Relying on His Grace = Restful

When you step into what God has called you to do and you're relying on His grace, you can't help but to experience that and change the world around you by His grace which is flowing through you.

Questions to Ponder

Is your daily life one of rest or is it a struggle?

Are you happy with your current vocation, career, job?

Have you experienced situations in which you know it was clearly the favor of God that worked on your behalf?

If so, what were those situations?

What steps can you take to step into your grace place?

Chapter 8
One Thing is Needful

Takeaways

We should never get so busy with our serving we fail to do what gives us the strength to serve in the first place, which is sitting at His feet.

My friend, you must take time to draw from Him.

Martha's focus was on what she must *do* for Jesus. Mary's focus was on Jesus himself.

When you realize you can do nothing without Him (John 15:5) your focus is on Him and receiving from that divine life. When you receive from Him, you are empowered to go and do.

We are refreshed in His presence when we're sitting at His feet.

My friend, all you need to do is simply come to Him to receive the refreshing for your soul.

Whether you choose to spend time at Jesus' feet by reading the word, praying in English or by praying in the Spirit the important thing is to take the time to receive from Him to get the refreshing your soul needs to effectively walk in your grace place.

Questions to Ponder

Do I regularly spend time sitting at Jesus' Feet?

How can I make time with Jesus a priority?

Chapter 9
Take Action

Here's your homework:

- Read and re-read the chapters in this book about how much God loves you and has qualified you.
- Listen to Jesus-filled sermons that impart grace.
- Meditate on scriptures that speak of His love for you and your righteousness in Christ.
- Spend time praying about where your grace place is. The Lord is faithful and will show you where it is you will flourish.
- If you already know where your grace place is, take steps in that direction.
- Whatever you "do", do it trusting and relying on Him and His grace.
- His grace is sufficient for you and will produce the desired results. It's your job to abide in Him, sit at His feet, and let His divine life flow through you to reach the world around you.

Questions to Ponder

What does this mean for me?

How can I apply this to my life?

What is the next action I need to take to implement this?

<u>NOTES</u>

NOTES

Made in the USA
San Bernardino, CA
21 December 2019

62182356R00053